Earthquakes
and Tsunamis

Emily Bone

Illustrated by Natalie Hinrichsen

Designed by Will Dawes, Lucy Wain and Zöe Wray

Additional illustrations by Nicola Slater

Earthquake consultant: Dr. Roger Trend

Reading consultant: Alison Kelly, Principal Lecturer at the University of Roehampton

Contents

3 Shaking earth
4 Moving rock
6 Faults
8 How does it feel?
10 Slipping land
12 City destruction
14 After the quake
16 Helping people
18 Earthquakes at sea
20 Tsunami warning
22 San Francisco shock
24 Staying safe
26 Earthquake drills
28 When will it happen?
30 Glossary
31 Websites to visit
32 Index

Shaking earth

During an earthquake, the ground suddenly trembles. Earthquakes can happen on land or under the sea.

Some earthquakes shake the ground violently. An earthquake has made the big cracks in these roads in Haiti.

Moving rock

The Earth is made of rock. Inside the Earth, there is very hot rock that moves around very, very slowly.

The Earth's surface is made up of big pieces of hard rock, called plates.

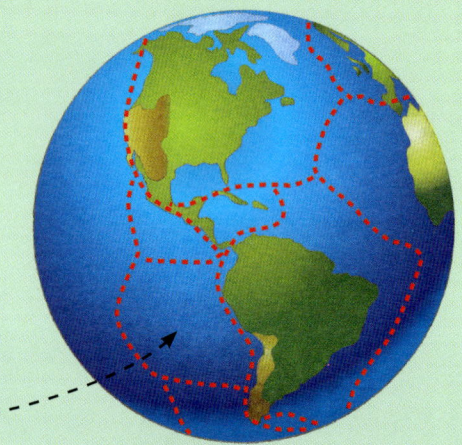

A plate

The plates move around on top of the hot rock.

As they move, some plates push against each other. Others pull apart.

When plates push against each other for millions of years, they form mountains.

Here are the edges of two plates in Iceland. The plates are moving away from each other, in opposite directions.

The gap made in the Earth's surface is called a rift.

Faults

Most earthquakes happen where two plates scrape against each other.

In some places there are cracks near the edges of the plates, called faults.

This is the San Andreas fault in California, U.S.A. Over 10,000 earthquakes happen along its length, every year.

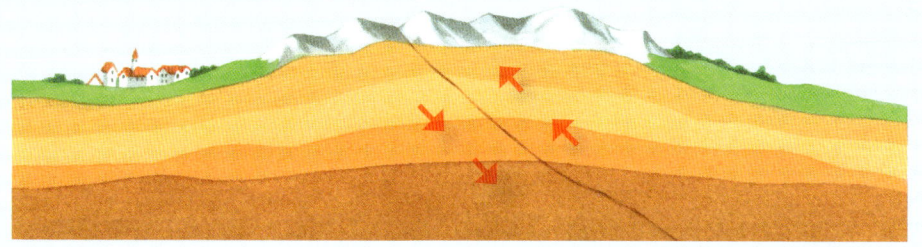

Sections of rock in a fault shift and push against each other.

Sometimes, a big section of rock suddenly slips, making the surrounding rock shake.

The shaking spreads up to the surface, causing an earthquake.

As the rock in a fault settles after a big earthquake it can cause smaller quakes, called aftershocks.

How does it feel?

When an earthquake starts, the ground trembles, then shakes violently. The effects of an earthquake are measured on a scale. The most famous is called the Richter scale.

0 means that the ground is completely still.

At levels 4 to 5, windows rattle. Things are thrown off shelves and walls.

At levels 6 and above, buildings may collapse and people are very frightened.

This road in Japan broke up during an earthquake at around level 6.

Thousands of earthquakes happen every year but most are so gentle that no one notices them.

Slipping land

Earthquakes also loosen big sections of soil and rock, making them slip down steep slopes. This is called a landslide.

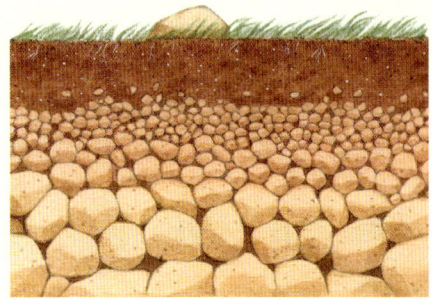 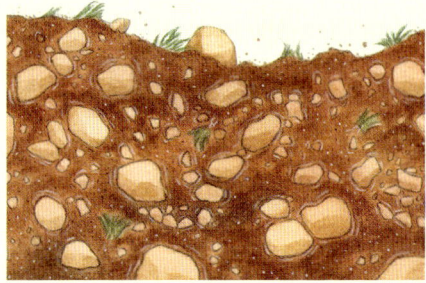

Usually, soil and rocks on the ground are packed closely together.

When the ground shakes, the rocks and soil are shaken apart.

On a slope, the loose rocks slide down very quickly, pushing more rocks and soil down, too.

Part of this hill in China has fallen away during a landslide. The rocks have smashed into houses at the bottom.

City destruction

When a big earthquake strikes in a city, it causes serious damage, and puts peoples' lives in danger.

Buildings are shaken in all directions, making their walls crack and collapse.

Electricity cables fall down, so people don't have any power, light or heat.

The trembling ground makes roads and bridges break up.

Water pipes burst open, cutting off water supplies to the city.

This is a city in Japan after a violent earthquake.

After the quake

Rescue teams find people who are trapped and in danger after an earthquake.

This rescuer is using a dog to find people under buildings that collapsed during an earthquake in Japan.

The dog can find people by smelling them.

Rescuers use equipment to free people quickly and safely.

A rescuer pushes a small camera on a long pole through the rubble.

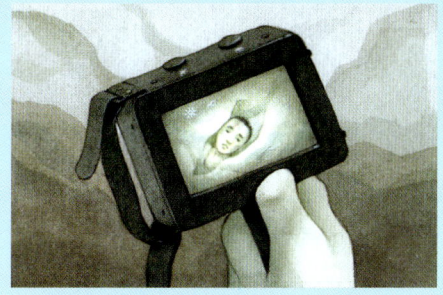

The camera is linked to a screen that shows if a person is trapped.

Rescuers carefully take away pieces of rubble to make a hole.

The person is lifted out of the hole and strapped onto a stretcher.

Helping people

When earthquakes damage houses and shops, people can be left with nowhere to live and no way to look after themselves.

To help people, emergency camps are set up, like this one in Pakistan. There are tents for people to sleep in.

People staying in the camp are given food, water, blankets and clothes.

Camp schools are set up so children don't miss their lessons.

Earthquakes at sea

When earthquakes happen under the sea they can create gigantic waves, called tsunamis. This is how they are made.

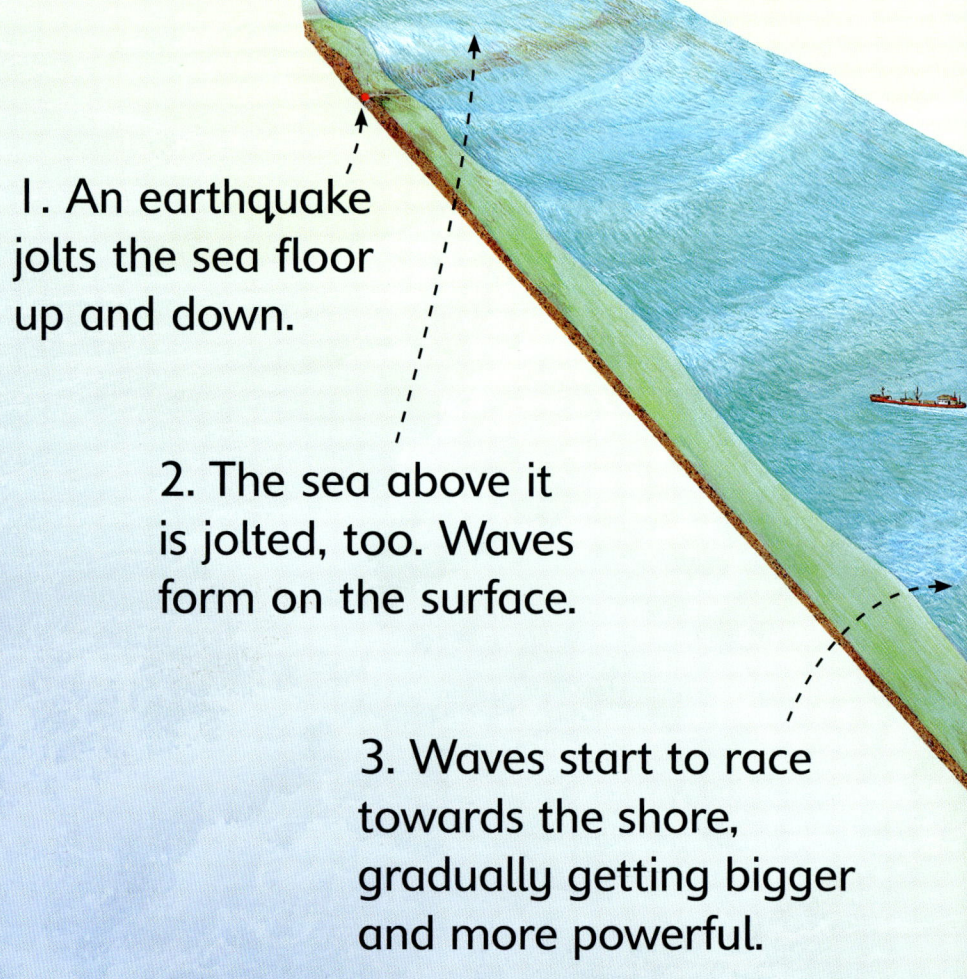

1. An earthquake jolts the sea floor up and down.

2. The sea above it is jolted, too. Waves form on the surface.

3. Waves start to race towards the shore, gradually getting bigger and more powerful.

Tsunamis are so powerful, they can carry huge ships far inland.

4. Massive waves crash onto the shore with enough force to destroy buildings and trees.

Tsunami warning

A tsunami can flood large areas of land.

Here, a tsunami in Indonesia has destroyed a village that is a long way from the sea.

In tsunami danger areas, there are warning systems to help people get to safety quickly.

Machines detect an earthquake at sea and send signals to a control room.

Computers in the control room find out where a tsunami may happen.

Alarms sound in the places in danger. People run to high ground.

San Francisco shock

San Francisco in California, U.S.A, is close to the San Andreas fault. On April 18, 1906, a major earthquake struck the city.

The shaking was so violent, many buildings collapsed. This photograph shows San Francisco a week after the earthquake.

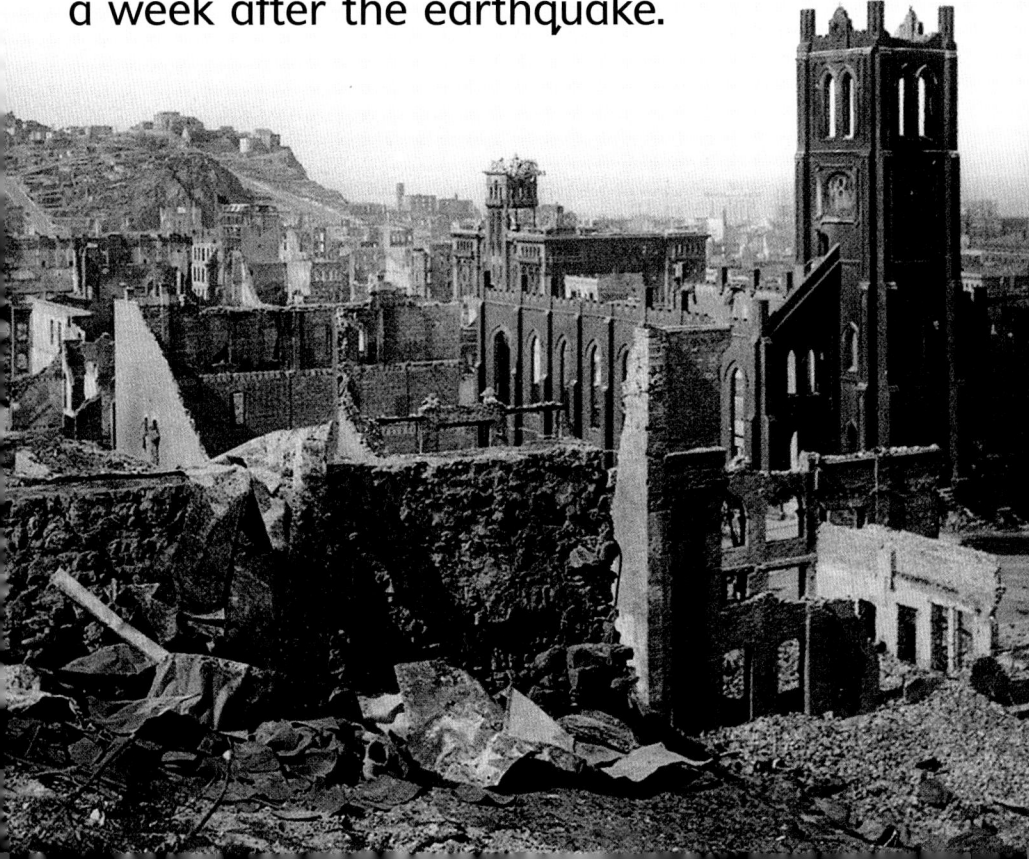

Power lines broke, causing huge fires that destroyed most of the city.

People who had lost their homes were moved to big, temporary camps.

Staying safe

In some areas where earthquakes happen, there are new ways to protect people during an earthquake.

Buildings are designed so that they don't collapse during earthquakes.

The walls of this skyscraper in Taiwan sway when the ground shakes, but they don't break apart.

Some houses are built on stilts to stop them from being flooded by tsunamis.

Here are some ways that people prepare so they can stay safe during an earthquake.

Heavy furniture is attached to walls so it doesn't fall over and hurt people.

Families arrange a safe place to meet in case they get split up.

People keep a kit of emergency supplies such as fresh water and blankets.

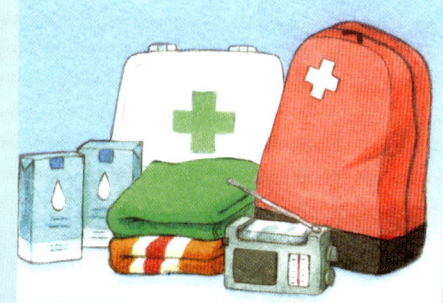

Earthquake drills

People living in danger of earthquakes rehearse what to do if an earthquake starts when they're at school or work.

These school children in Japan are learning how to shelter under their desks. This would stop them from being hurt by falling objects.

For the next part of the drill, the children calmly walk out of the building in a line.

They wear padded hoods as this would protect their heads during an earthquake.

Everyone gathers in an open space, away from trees and buildings.

They crouch down so they wouldn't be knocked over if the ground shook.

When will it happen?

No one knows for certain when or where an earthquake will happen.

Scientists study faults as they think movements in the rock may help them to predict earthquakes.

Here, scientists are using powerful beams of light to detect any movement.

Some people believe that there are other ways to predict an earthquake.

Sometimes, dogs bark and run outside just before an earthquake starts.

Frogs and other animals may leave an area days before an earthquake hits.

Flashes of light in the sky could mean an earthquake is about to happen.

Glossary

Here are some of the words in this book you might not know. This page tells you what they mean.

 plate - a big piece of moving rock. Plates make up the Earth's surface.

 faults - cracks in the rock along plate edges where earthquakes happen.

 landslide - when big sections of soil and rocks slip downhill.

 emergency camp - a place people can stay if their homes are destroyed.

 tsunami - massive waves formed when there is an earthquake at sea.

 warning system - a system to detect tsunamis so people can get to safety.

 earthquake drill - a rehearsal of what to do during and after an earthquake.

Websites to visit

You can visit exciting websites to find out more about earthquakes and tsunamis.

To visit these websites, go to the Usborne Quicklinks Website at **www.usborne-quicklinks.com** Read the internet safety guidelines, and then type the keywords "**beginners earthquakes**".

The websites are regularly reviewed and the links in Usborne Quicklinks are updated. However, Usborne Publishing is not responsible, and does not accept liability, for the content or availability of any website other than its own. We recommend that children are supervised while on the internet.

A powerful tsunami in Indonesia washed these houses onto a beach.

Index

animals, 14, 29
buildings, 9, 11, 12, 13, 14, 16, 19, 20, 22, 23, 24, 25, 27, 31
camps, 16-17, 23, 30
cities, 12-13, 22, 23
detection, 21, 28-29
drills, 26-27, 30
Earth, 4, 5
emergency supplies, 17, 25
faults, 6-7, 22, 28, 30
flooding, 20, 25
landslides, 10-11, 30
people, 9, 14, 15, 16, 17, 21, 23, 24, 25, 26, 27
plates, 4-5, 6, 30
power, 12, 23
rescue teams, 14-15
roads, 3, 9, 13
rocks, 4, 7, 10, 11, 28
safety, 15, 21, 24-25, 26, 27
schools, 17, 26
sea, 3, 18, 19, 20, 21
shaking, 3, 7, 8, 12, 13, 24, 27
tsunamis, 18-19, 20, 21, 25, 30, 31

Acknowledgements

Photographic manipulation by Nick Wakeford
With thanks to Ruth King and Sam Lake

Photo credits

The publishers are grateful to the following for permission to reproduce material: cover © **TWPhoto/Corbis**; p1 © **2011 AFP/Getty**; p2-3 © **Robert Harding World Imagery/Alamy**; p5 © **Robert Harding Travel/Photolibrary (Geoff Renner)**; p6 © **Peter Arnold Images/Photolibrary (Kevin Schafer)**; p 8 © **Kyodo/X01481/Reuters/Corbis**; p9 © **Niigata-Nippo/Hiroshi Sekine/Reuters/Corbis**; p11 © **Jason Lee/Reuters/Corbis**; p12-13 © **Michael S. Yamashita/Corbis**; p14 © **Ria Novosti**; p16-17 © **Goran Tomasevic/Reuters/Corbis**; p18-19, p30 (tsunami entry) © **Gary Hinks/Science Photo Library**; p20 © **Stephen J. Boitano/Alamy**; p22-23 © **US National Archive, 111-AGF-1A-1D**; p24 © **Tom Bonaventure/Getty**; p26 © **AFP/Getty Images**; p29 © **David Parker/Science Photo Library**; p31 © **Trinity Mirror/Mirrorpix/Alamy**.

Every effort has been made to trace and acknowledge ownership of copyright. If any rights have been omitted, the publishers offer to rectify this in any subsequent editions following notification.

First published in 2012 by Usborne Publishing Ltd., Usborne House, 83-85 Saffron Hill, London EC1N 8RT, England. www.usborne.com Copyright © 2012 Usborne Publishing Ltd. The name Usborne and the devices ⚑ are Trade Marks of Usborne Publishing Ltd. All rights reserved. No part of this publication may be reproduced, stored in a retrieval system, or transmitted in any form or by any means, electronic, mechanical, photocopying, recording or otherwise without the prior permission of the publisher. First published in America 2012. U.E.